THE STORY OF CINCO DE MAYO

BY MAXIMILIAN SMITH

 Gareth Stevens
PUBLISHING

Please visit our website, www.garethstevens.com. For a free color catalog of all our high-quality books, call toll free 1-800-542-2595 or fax 1-877-542-2596.

Library of Congress Cataloging-in-Publication Data

Smith, Maximilian, author.
 The story of Cinco de Mayo / Maximilian Smith.
     pages cm. — (The history of our holidays)
 Includes bibliographical references and index.
ISBN 978-1-4824-3898-7 (pbk.)
ISBN 978-1-4824-3899-4 (6 pack)
ISBN 978-1-4824-3900-7 (library binding)
1. Cinco de Mayo (Mexican holiday)—Juvenile literature. 2. Puebla, Battle of, Puebla de Zaragoza, Mexico, 1862—Juvenile literature. I. Title.
 F1233.S67 2016
 394.262—dc23
                                        2015018172

Published in 2016 by
Gareth Stevens Publishing
111 East 14th Street, Suite 349
New York, NY 10003

Designer: Sarah Liddell
Editor: Therese Shea

Photo credits: Cover, p. 1 Kobby Dagan/Shutterstock.com; p. 5 Fer Gregory/ Shutterstock.com; p. 7 meraklitasarim/Shutterstock.com; p. 9 (Juarez) Afernand74/ Wikimedia Commons; p. 9 (Napoleon III) Testus/Wikimedia Commons; p. 11 Gusvel/Wikimedia Commons; p. 13 De Agostini/G. Dagli Orti/De Agostini Picture Library/Getty Images; p. 15 Xiuhtecuhtli-commonswiki/Wikimedia Commons; p. 17 Ruiz~commonswiki/Wikimedia Commons; p. 19 Susana Gonzalez/Stringer/Getty Images News/Getty Images; p. 21 Gary Conner/Photolibrary/Getty Images.

Printed in the United States of America

CPSIA compliance information: Batch #CW16GS: For further information contact Gareth Stevens, New York, New York at 1-800-542-2595.

CONTENTS

May 5 4

The Battle of Puebla 8

Cinco de Mayo Today 16

Glossary 22

For More Information 23

Index 24

Boldface words appear in the glossary.

May 5

Each year on May 5, you may see many green, red, and white flags. You may see Mexican foods at stores and restaurants, too. Many people love to **celebrate** the holiday called Cinco de Mayo (SEEN-koh DEH MY-oh).

Cinco de Mayo is Spanish for "fifth of May." This was an important day in the history of Mexico. On May 5, 1862, the Mexican army **defeated** French forces at a battle in a small town in Mexico called Puebla de Los Angeles.

The Battle of Puebla

In 1862, French **emperor** Napoleon III sent an army to collect money Mexico **owed** France. Mexican president Benito Juarez said Mexico had no money to pay France. The French started marching toward Mexico City to take control of the country.

Napoleon III

Benito Juarez

9

On May 5, about 6,000 French **troops** met about 4,000 Mexican troops near the town of Puebla de Los Angeles. Many of the Mexican soldiers weren't really soldiers. They were farmworkers armed with old guns and knives.

The French general was sure that his soldiers could easily beat the Mexicans. He ordered his forces to attack the middle of the Mexican army. This was the Mexicans' strongest point. The French had to march up Guadalupe Hill and cross a **ditch**.

13

By the time the French reached the Mexicans, they were tired. The Mexican soldiers, led by General Ignacio Zaragoza, were ready for them. About 1,000 French soldiers died. Finally, the French general ordered his troops to **retreat**.

15

Cinco de Mayo Today

The Mexican win at Puebla de Los Angeles is why people celebrate Cinco de Mayo. The proud Mexicans had beaten the powerful French army. Today, Puebla de Los Angeles is called Puebla de Zaragoza to honor the general.

General
Ignacio Zaragoza

17

The state of Puebla holds the largest Cinco de Mayo celebration in Mexico today. There are parades, speeches, and a very special way of remembering what happened. People dress as Mexican and French soldiers and act out the battle.

In the United States, Cinco de Mayo celebrations include Mexican music, dancing, and food. The largest **festivals** are in the cities of Los Angeles, Chicago, and Houston. Mexican Americans and many others celebrate the Mexican **culture** each year on May 5. You should, too!

GLOSSARY

celebrate: to honor with special activities

culture: the beliefs and ways of life of a group of people

defeat: to beat

ditch: a long narrow path dug in the ground

emperor: a man who rules an empire, or a group of nations

festival: a special time when something is celebrated

owe: to need to pay money to someone

retreat: to withdraw or move away after a defeat

troops: a number of soldiers

FOR MORE INFORMATION

BOOKS

Gnojewski, Carol. *Celebrating Cinco de Mayo*. Berkeley Heights, NJ: Enslow Elementary, 2012.

Tait, Leia. *Cinco de Mayo*. New York, NY: Smartbook Media, 2016.

WEBSITES

Cinco de Mayo
www.history.com/topics/holidays/cinco-de-mayo
Read about the battle that is remembered each year on May 5.

Cinco de Mayo Activities for Kids and Teachers
www.kiddyhouse.com/Holidays/Cinco/
Read more about this holiday and find links to crafts and activities.

INDEX

Chicago 20

dancing 20

foods 4, 20

France 8

French 6, 8, 10, 12,
     14, 16, 18

Guadalupe Hill 12

Houston 20

Juarez, Benito 8

Los Angeles 20

Mexican 4, 6, 8, 10,
     12, 14, 16, 18, 20

Mexico 6, 8, 18

music 20

Napoleon III 8

parades 18

Puebla de Los
     Angeles 6, 10, 16

Puebla de Zaragoza
     16

speeches 18

Zaragoza, Ignacio 14